YOU KNOW YOU'RE FROM BUFFALO IF...

ADAM ZYGLIS

MacIntyre Purcell Publishing Inc.

MacIntyre Purcell Publishing Inc.
194 Hospital Rd.
Lunenburg, Nova Scotia
B0J 2C0
(902) 640-3350

www.macintyrepurcell.com
info@macintyrepurcell.com

Printed and bound in Canada by Friesens
Design and layout: Channel Communications and Gwen North

ISBN978-1-77276-161-0 (softcover)

Library and Archives Canada Cataloguing in Publication

Title: You know you're from Buffalo if... / by Adam Zyglis.
Other titles: You know you are from Buffalo if...
Names: Zyglis, Adam, author. Identifiers: Canadiana 2021022794X | ISBN 9781772761610 (softcover)
Subjects: LCSH: Buffalo (N.Y.)—Social life and customs—Caricatures and cartoons. | LCSH: Wit and humor, Pictorial. | LCGFT: Comics (Graphic works)
Classification: LCC F129.B84 Z94 2021 | DDC 974.7/9700207—dc23

FOR CLYDE and VERA

INTRODUCTION

I was born and raised in Buffalo, as they say. I grew up in rural Alden, with my parents hailing from the working-class neighborhoods of Cheektowaga and West Seneca. I moved to the city to attend Canisius College, and to explore the urban side of Western New York. In the years since, I've lived in neighborhoods around the city and ventured to the far corners of our region. I'm proud to say this is my stomping ground.

Being a Buffalonian is like having a sacredly held heirloom… full of stories and paradoxes. It's equal parts disappointment and hope, pride and insecurity, grit and sophistication. It's that feeling in your bones when the waterfront winds shake you, when the arena rumbles with a Sabres overtime win, and when you're hit with too much horseradish on a beef on weck. And when you meet other Buffalonians out in the world, you have an instant kinship, knowing they get it all.

Producing this book has been therapeutic — a much-needed release of the built up Buffalo ethos in my system. It's also been a much-needed break from politics, and a return to my roots.

I'd like to thank everyone who helped me piece together these pages. To all my friends and family and coworkers, thank you for your feedback and suggestions. Most importantly, thank you to my wife, Jessica, for providing your brilliant fresh set of eyes, and for putting up with many late nights and holding down the fort!

ADAM ZYGUS

YOU KNOW YOU'RE FROM BUFFALO IF...

...AND HEART PROBLEMS...

ZYGUS

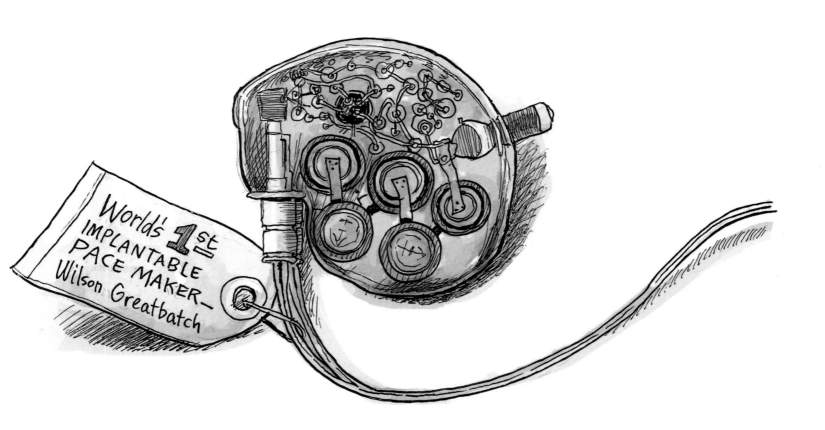

World's **1**st IMPLANTABLE PACE MAKER — Wilson Greatbatch

...AND HEART SOLUTIONS.

YOU PUT "THE" IN FRONT OF HIGHWAY NAMES

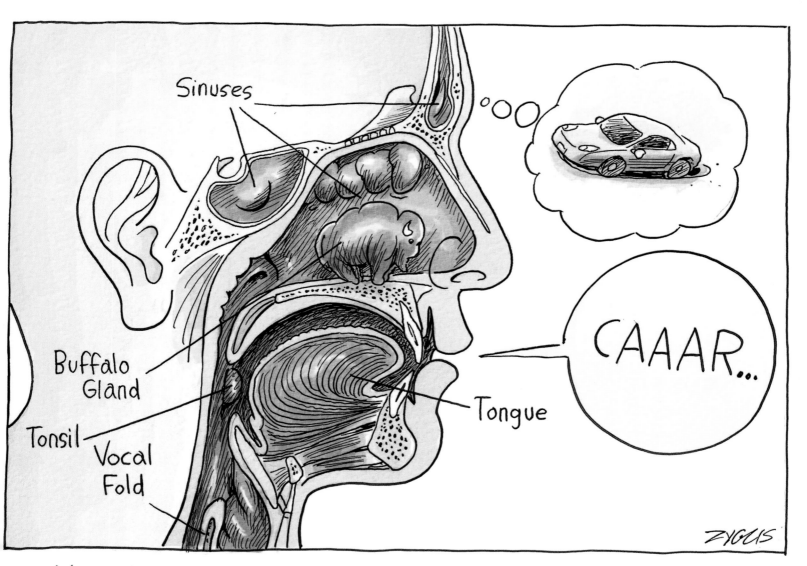

YOUR LOCAL ACCENT SOUNDS Like A SINUS INFECTION...

PEOPLE FROM other COUNTRIES think YOU'RE FROM NYC...

PEOPLE FROM NYC think YOU'RE FROM A DAIRY FARM IN the ADIRONDACKS

"THE HIP" IS MUCH MORE THAN...

...JUST A PART OF YOUR BODY.

16

THERE'S NO PLACE YOU'D RATHER BE THAN RIGHT HERE RIGHT NOW.

YOUR FIRST THREE CAVITIES WERE A DIRECT RESULT OF TOO MUCH LOGANBERRY

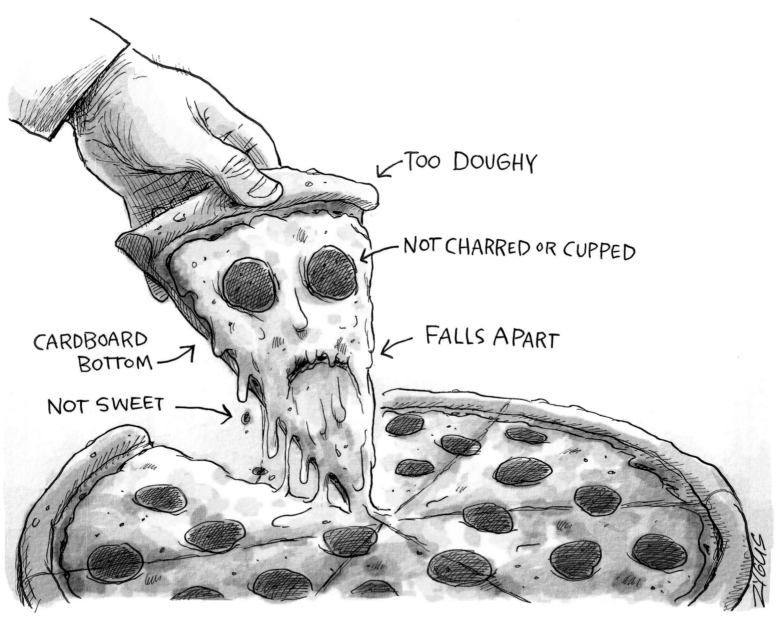

PIZZA FROM ANY OTHER US CITY IS JUST SAD...

THIS IS
HOW YOU
GIVE A
NEW
ENGLAND
PATRIOTS
FAN
Table
Service
↳→

YOUR HOMETOWN'S TRUE Culinary KING IS OVERSHADOWED BY the WING

YOU BUY REAL ESTATE BASED ON YOUR SNOW TOTAL TOLERANCE...

ZYODS

YOU KEEP this IN YOUR CAR YEAR ROUND.

"WIDE RIGHT" IS AKIN TO A SWEAR WORD...

YOU EARN A SCARLET LETTER FOR DIPPING YOUR WINGS IN RANCH...

THE NAMES...

SULLIVAN,

RICHARDSON,

AND WRIGHT...

INSPIRE AWE.

ZYGLIS

YOUR CITY SMELLS MAGICALLY DELICIOUS...

"TOP SHELF" isn't really "WHERE MAMA HIDES THE COOKIES"

The BILLS MAKE YOU WANNA...

SEASONAL AFFECTIVE DISORDER IS FOR REAL.

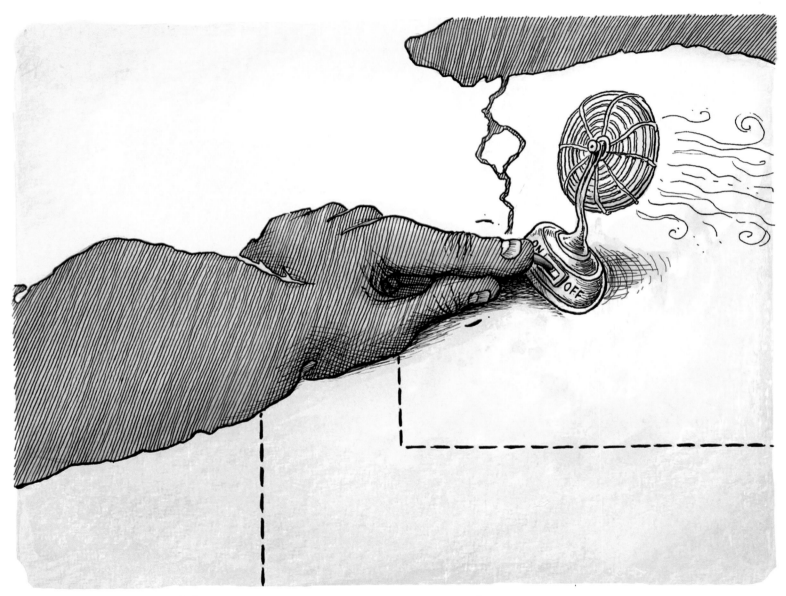

YOUR LAKE COOLS YOU IN the SUMMER...

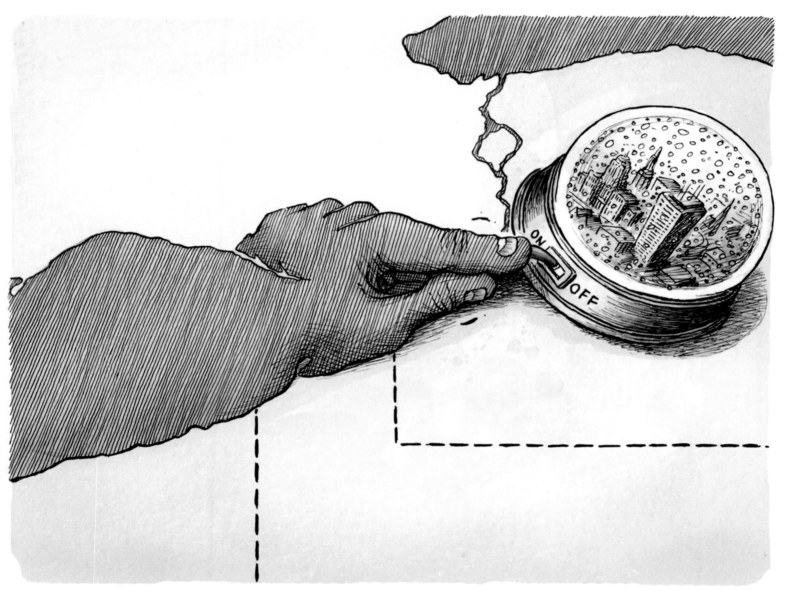

...AND FOOLS YOU IN the WINTER.

YOUR ART DECO *Masterpiece* OF A CITY HALL INSPIRED the GHOSTBUSTERS BUILDING.

CLIMATE CHANGE IS ACTUALLY MAKING YOUR TOWN MORE ATTRACTIVE...

HOUSES of WORSHIP CAN BECOME ENTERTAINMENT Venues...

ENTERTAINMENT Venues CAN BECOME HOUSES of WORSHIP.

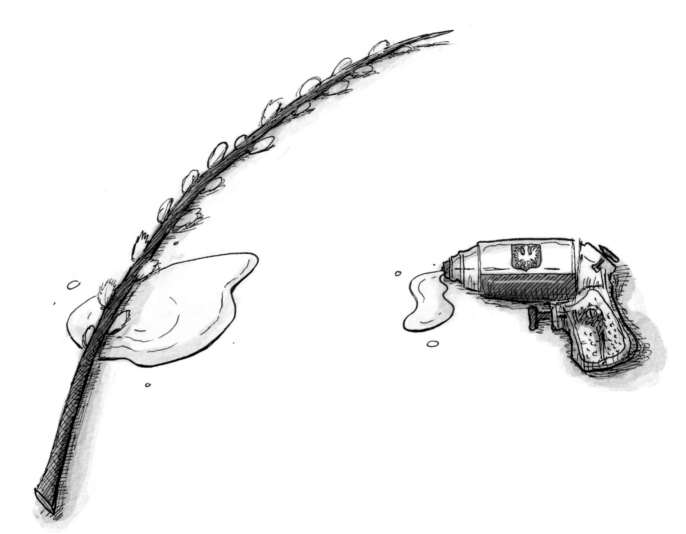

YOU KNOW EXACTLY WHAT To Do with A PUSSYWILLOW and A SQUIRT GUN.

YOU LOOK at YOUR CITY the WAY JOSH ALLEN LOOKS at STEFON DIGGS.

A PARENTING RITE of PASSAGE IS *threatening* "FATHER BAKERS"

THE SIGHT of SNOW DOES NOT SCARE YOU...

YOU CAN PADDLE *through* THE WORLD'S LARGEST COLLECTION *of* GRAIN ELEVATORS.

YOU CAN BOOGIE *through* THE WORLD'S LARGEST DISCO.

WHAT HAPPENS IN CHEEKTOVEGAS *Stays* IN CHEEKTOVEGAS

MARCH COMES IN LIKE A LION and OUT LIKE A BUTTER LAMB...

ZYGUS

The BEST STEAK SANDWICH YOU EVER HAD was AT 1:30AM AT THE PINK.

YOUR PARENTS SPENT HALF their RETIREMENT ON YOUR YOUTH LEAGUE...

THE SUN GOES MISSING FROM OCTOBER to APRIL...

YOU CAN ENJOY WEST COAST SUNSETS *without the* WEST COAST TRAFFIC...

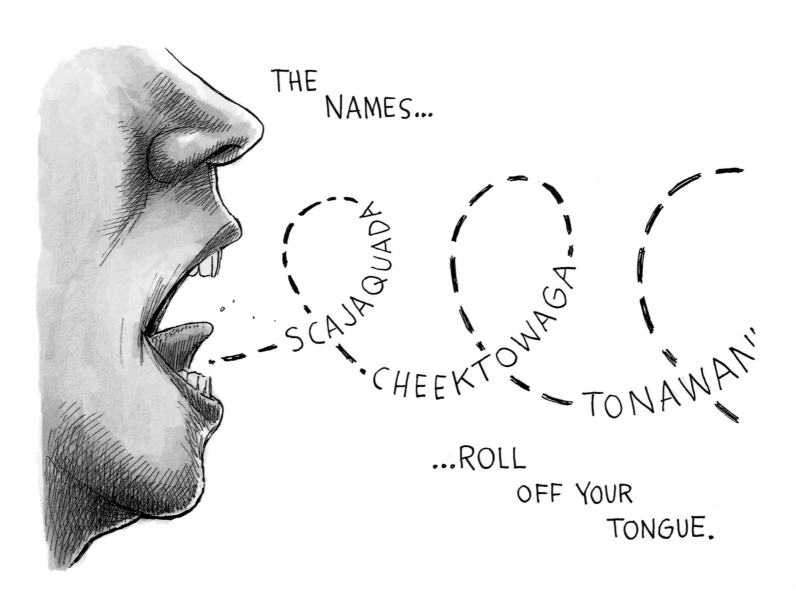

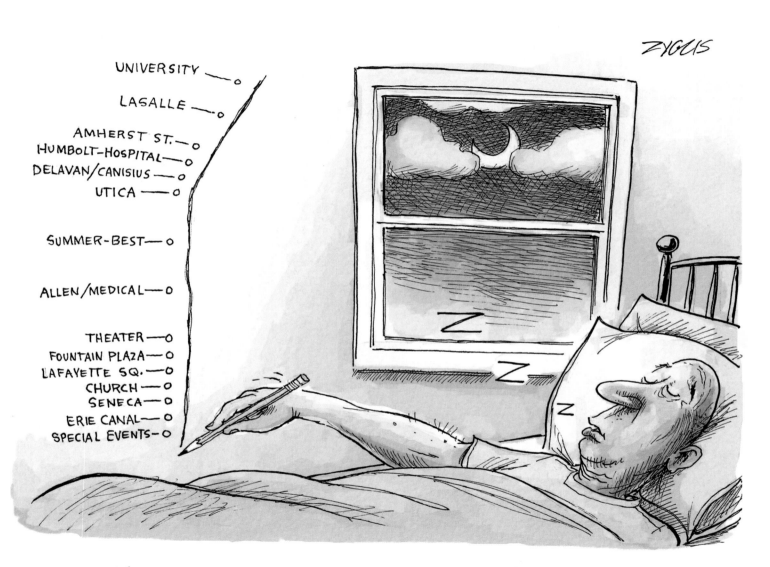

YOU CAN DRAW YOUR CITY'S SUBWAY MAP IN YOUR SLEEP...

YOU'RE ON A FIRST NAME BASIS with YOUR FAVORITE COMFORT FOODS...

YOU WILL FOREVER CALL IT...

YOU DUMP SEWAGE and WASTE INTO YOUR WATERWAYS...

'GOING to THE BEACH' LITERALLY JUST MEANS GOING to the BEACH...

EVERY JULY YOU GET GARDEN INFERIORITY COMPLEX...

ZYGLIS

YOU DON'T CONSIDER THESE TO BE IMPORTS...

A GLOBAL PANDEMIC CANNOT STOP YOUR TAILGATE TRADITION...

You KNOW every WORD To the NATIONAL ANTHEM...

...OF CANADA.

ZYGLIS

THE WORLD-CLASS WATER FEATURE IN YOUR BACKYARD IS NBD...

You know every word to the conehead guarantee...

YOUR GO-TO _____ GIFT FOR _____.
(insert Holiday)   (extended family member)

ZYGUS

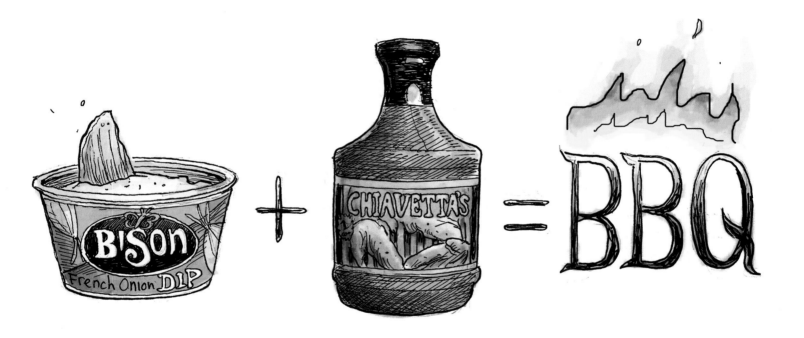

THIS *always* ADDS UP...

BEING A PART of A 'MAFIA' HIT JOB...

IS ACTUALLY A GOOD THING.

ZYGAS

YOU GET A BIT DEFENSIVE WHEN OTHERS DIS YOUR CITY...

The Words...

"PIZZA" + "LOGS"

Go Together *like*

"THUNDER" + "SNOW"

ZYGUS

EVERY FIZZY SUGARY DRINK IS CALLED

WHEN TRAVELING, YOU'RE REQUIRED to GREET EVERYONE from BUFFALO WITH:

YOUR CITY'S IMMIGRANTS UNITE US...

YOU'RE SLOWLY ROLLING BACK YOUR HISTORIC BLUNDERS ...

YOU'RE ALWAYS BOASTING OF YOUR HISTORIC TRIUMPHS.

YOU KNOW WHERE McKINLEY WAS SHOT...

YOU KNOW WHERE TR WAS SWORN IN...

THESE TWO LITERARY GIANTS SPENT FORMATIVE YEARS IN YOUR CITY...

The BEST SNOWSTORM ADVICE YOU GOT WAS TO "GRAB A SIX-PACK"

YOUR FAVORITE
WINTER JEANS
HAVE THAT...

...STUBBORN TELLTALE
SALT STAIN.

ZYGLIS

YOU FEEL LIKE A KID EVERY TIME YOU SEE ALLENTOWN'S BUBBLEMAN.

YOU FEEL LIKE A KID EVERY TIME YOU ENTER VIDLER'S 5 & 10.

ZYGUS

CHRISTMAS isn't CHRISTMAS UNTIL YOU GIFT YOURSELF ONE of THESE...

YOU'RE A SUPER FREAK...

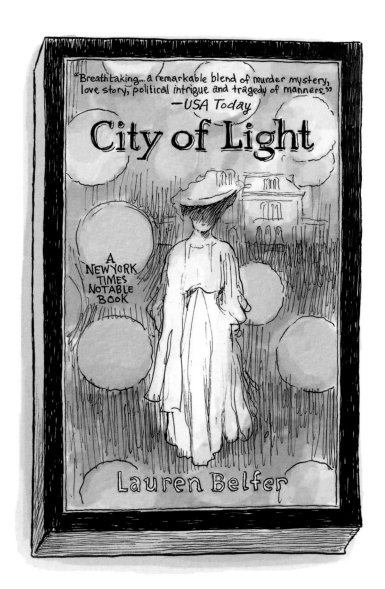

YOU HAVE *this* IN YOUR LIBRARY...

YOU HAVE this IN YOUR DVD COLLECTION...

THE FISH FRY IS KIND OF A "BIG DEAL"...

"Buffalo buffalo Buffalo buffalo buffalo buffalo Buffalo buffalo"

YOUR CITY IS A HOMONYM...

YOU'VE SUFFERED THROUGH 16 YEARS OF THIS...

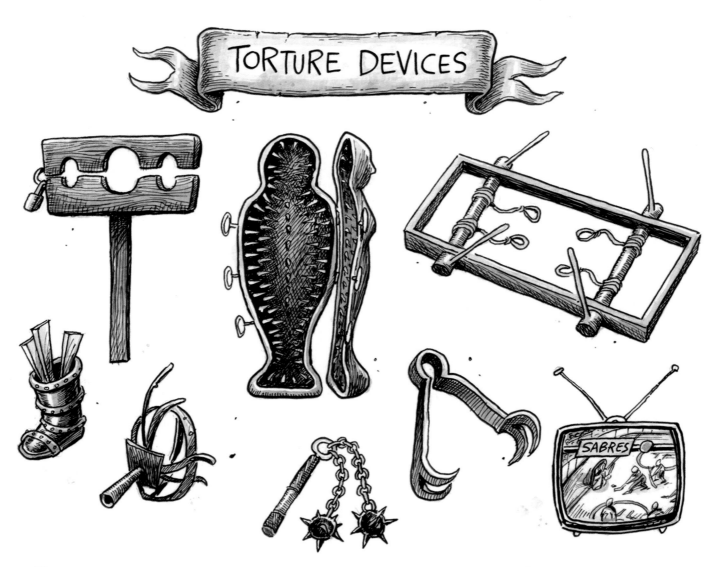

TORTURE DEVICES

BEING A HOCKEY FAN BRINGS OUT YOUR MASOCHISM...

YOU ASSOCIATE FRANK LLOYD WRIGHT ARCHITECTURE with LONG HORIZONTAL LINES

YOUR TOWN'S RESURGENCE IS A TALE OF TWO CITIES...

THE BLIZZARD of '77 KICKED YOUR DUPA...

YOU'VE TRIED SMUGGLING THESE THROUGH AIRPORT SECURITY...

YOUR BIGGEST MUSIC MEMORIES WERE MADE in the SMALLEST of SPACES.

YOU'RE _100%_ IRISH ON ST. PADDY'S DAY...

YOU'RE _100%_ POLISH ON DYNGUS DAY.

FRENCH TRAPPERS MAY HAVE INSPIRED YOUR CITY'S NAME...

... THE FRENCH CONNECTION ADDED to ITS FAME.

YOU ALWAYS HAVE A PATH SHOVELED to THE GRILL.

YOU PUT A BUFFALO ON EVERYTHING.

YOUR CITY INVENTED COOL...

THE END.